Cesar Chavez

A Hero for Everyone

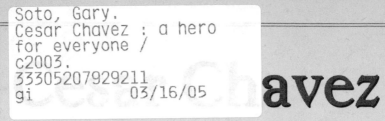

Cesar Chavez

A Hero for Everyone

BY GARY SOTO

ILLUSTRATED BY LORI LOHSTOETER

New York   Singapore

First Aladdin Paperbacks edition September 2003
Text copyright © 2003 by Gary Soto
Illustrations copyright © 2003 by Lori Lohstoeter

ALADDIN PAPERBACKS
An imprint of Simon & Schuster Children's Publishing Division
1230 Avenue of the Americas
New York, NY 10020

Also available in an Aladdin Library edition.
Designed by Debra Sfetsios
The text of this book was set in Cheltenham.

Printed in the United States of America
2 4 6 8 10 9 7 5 3

Library of Congress Control Number 2003103043
ISBN 0-689-85922-8

In memory of Peter Velasco

CHAPTER ONE

Seeing for Himself

IN HIS 1953 Mercury station wagon, Cesar Chavez pulled into Corcoran, California. It was late summer, 1962. With a few other recruiters from the organization he would later call the National Farm Workers Association (NFWA), he was there to go door to door, telling farmworkers about a new union that would help them.

Corcoran was a small California valley town of about five thousand people. Most of these people were Mexican Americans. They were poor and often lived in barrios or labor camps. They worked in the fields that surrounded Corcoran, harvesting grapes in the summer and picking cotton in the fall.

Corcoran had a history of labor problems. In 1933 it had been the site of a farmworkers' strike. The cotton pickers were paid by piecework. This meant that they didn't get paid by the hour but by how much they picked. The pickers were asking for better pay and fairness from the farmers, who occasionally cheated them. If you picked cotton, you dragged a sack—or "sacko," in Spanglish— until it was so full it was too heavy to drag anymore. Then a farmer or his foreman would weigh the sack. Sometimes farmers would trick the workers with scales that weren't properly balanced. Other times they might fire a worker for resting for ten minutes. This worker was usually fired at the end of the day, and he would only get a portion of his wages, never what he deserved.

Cesar was only six when the strike broke out, but later as young man he read and heard about it. He knew that the strikers had been beaten and shot and sometimes killed by armed farmers.

Cesar did have personal memories of Corcoran. When he was a boy, his family used to travel up and down California's Central Valley looking for work. One summer, in the early 1940s, they stopped in Corcoran to pick cotton. But the contractor, the person who hired the workers and was responsible for paying them, ran off with their hard-earned money.

Now Cesar walked from house to house. He introduced himself in Spanish. He explained to the person who came to the door—a man or woman who was tired from working in the field—about the desperate need for justice for the farmworker.

"What is it you want?" a man might ask.

Cesar's answer would be that he wanted to start a movement to make life better for farmworkers.

By 1965 Chicanos—Mexican Americans—would call that movement simply, *la causa*, the cause to change how farmworkers were treated. The cause, also, to change how all Mexican Americans were treated in small rural towns and in the larger cities.

"¡Viva la causa!" would become the chant of the farmworker.

CHAPTER TWO

Beginnings

CESAR'S DESIRE TO fight injustice probably started when he was ten years old. His family lost its 118-acre farm outside of Yuma, Arizona, when the Chavez family couldn't afford to pay the taxes they owed on it. His mother, Juana, may have influenced him. Every October 16 she honored St. Eduvigis, a Polish duchess, who gave away all her worldly goods to the poor. Or it may have begun with the stories of his very strong and hardworking grandfather, Cesario, for whom he was named. Cesario had escaped in the late 1880s from a hacienda in the

Mexican state of Chihuahua. All of these influences created at the core of Cesar's heart a tenderness for the poor.

Cesar was born on March 31, 1927, upstairs from the Chavez family store. The store sold food and other items that farmers and farmworkers needed to work the land. But because business was slow, Cesar's father, Librado, had to sell his store. Cesar was five at the time. The family moved back to the farm that Cesar's grandfather Cesario, also known as Papa Chayo, had home-steaded for more than three decades. There they raised cotton but also had small plots of watermelon, corn, squash, and chilies. Chickens roamed in the shade of their adobe house.

Cesar rose early to do his chores and then trudged along with his sister, Rita, and brother, Richard, to a three-room schoolhouse. This was especially hard in winter when Cesar had nothing warmer to wear than a sweater.

School was an unwelcoming place. He wasn't allowed to speak Spanish, the family's household language. In fact speaking it brought on punishment. All Cesar would remember of school was the whistling of the ruler as it came down on his wrist or knuckles.

Cesar and Richard weren't above playing hooky. Once when the two boys skipped school, the principal drove to their home and reported them. They thought the desert was hot, but not nearly as hot as their bottoms after their father found out.

When the children weren't in school, they played in the trees with their homemade toys and made stick bridges over streams of water carved from the irrigation canals. They also helped in the fields. In spring they chopped cotton with a hoe. They then picked it in September. There were plenty of chores, and Cesar, like most children, complained to his father more than once. What child wouldn't complain about having to wake up at four in the morning to pick cotton on days when the temperature would rise to 110 degrees—even in the shade!

During the 1930s the whole country was suffering from the Great Depression. The average person didn't have enough money to live. There were few jobs. People went hungry.

As the Depression got worse, Cesar and Richard took baskets of eggs to neighbors and traded them for flour or cornmeal. In normal times the family could get five or six cents for a dozen eggs. But now no one, especially farmers, had any money jingling in their pockets. Because no one had money, neighbors did a lot of trading of goods. If a neighbor's goat was butchered, the Chavez family might get some of the meat in exchange for what they grew.

With millions out of work the mood of the country changed. It was certainly felt by the Chavez family. Things got worse when the North Gila Valley, where their farm was, suffered a drought. It seldom rained even in normal seasons. Everyone grew worried when their life source, the canal that ran in front of their house, shriveled to a trickle.

Cesar saw deep worry lines in his father's face. How would they live? It was about this time that Cesar and Richard got their first paying job. They hunted the gophers that not only harmed the local crops but also ruined the walls of the irrigation canals. For each gopher they trapped—they had to show the tail of the dead gopher—they got a penny.

At the start of each day, the boys would go out in search of what they considered valuable vermin. It wasn't a time to play. When Cesar grew up, he protected animals and would never hurt them. But during those early poor years, he and Richard were just trying to help their family.

CHAPTER THREE

On the Road with Others

BUT THE PENNIES they earned couldn't save the family farm. In 1938 Librado traveled to Oxnard, California, to work in the bean fields and wrote soon after for his family to join him. They said good-bye to their adobe house on the farm they no longer owned. They loaded up the car and joined the great mass of nearly a million people in search of work—any work—in California and the Northwest.

After a week on the road the Chavez family was in Oxnard. Imagine what Cesar thought of the fog shrouding the coastal town. He had never seen the ocean before, either. It was exciting for the ten-year-old boy to run backward from the waves lapping the beach. California was nothing like the Arizona desert.

But the fun was brief. During the next three months the family traveled up and down California in search of work—Atascadero, Gonzales, Salinas, and Half Moon Bay were a few of their stops. They slept in makeshift tents, in their car, or, if they got lucky, in someone's garage or backyard. At times they found some work, but not always. It was a difficult time for the Chavez family.

They settled for a while in San José's barrio called *Sal Si Puedes* ("Get Out if You Can"). The name said it all. It was a gritty place with unpaved roads, no sewers, no streetlights, canals choked with garbage and sewage from factories, and houses leaning crookedly on their brick foundations.

The residents were Mexicans who worked in the nearby fields and canneries. The crops were mostly cherries, prunes, plums, and apricots. These crops had to be picked quickly, boxed, and shipped. The cannery workers sorted tomatoes and peaches from the San Joaquin Valley by the truckload.

Sometimes Librado and Juana found work, but not often. And the work they did get, didn't pay much.

Cesar and Richard found odd jobs. They would crack walnuts, collect bottles and copper for the junk man, and chop wood for neighbors. They worked for pennies, which they gave to their mother, just as their father turned over his pay when he had work. The two boys splurged occasionally to see a movie, but they soon got wise and convinced the manager of the movie house to pay them to sweep up spilled popcorn during intermission.

That way they got to see the Lone Ranger movies for free, plus earn a little money.

They left San José after all the prunes were picked and worked their way down California to the Oxnard area. At each stop Juana would make the children enroll at the nearby school, even if only for a few days. She would argue as she ran a brush through her daughter Rita's hair: "I didn't learn, but you can learn, so you have to go."

Cesar didn't like school because people made fun of his Spanish accent. Plus he was aware that his clothes, while clean, were tattered and full of holes. Forget about style! Even his socks caused him ridicule. He seldom had a pair that matched. He stopped wearing socks when, in winter, of all times, his shoes fell apart. He had to go to school barefoot. The shame of walking into a classroom with mud between your toes!

Later Cesar and his brothers and sisters counted the schools they had attended. During a five-year period traveling up and down California, from the Pacific coast to the blazing desert, they had gone to about thirty-seven schools. And for what? Cesar would go no higher than the eighth grade.

More often than not Cesar joined his parents in the field. He had to help the family, for they were hungry and broke. He took up grape knives to slash at bunches of grapes, hoes for beets and cotton plants, sacks for onions, knives to pit apricots, poles to shake walnuts, stringy grass to tie carrots, machetes to top beets, hatchets to nail down the crates of cantaloupes, and ladders to lean against fruit trees dusted with pesticides. Bent over, he poked onion seeds into rows—one seed every four inches. During harvesttime, he worked an average of fourteen hours a day.

The schemes of the contractor, the man who hired the workers, were not always honorable. When he hired field-workers by the hour, he might cheat them ten minutes here, fifteen minutes there—these minutes added up if the contractor had a large crew. The time not reported was money in his pocket.

Or maybe the contractor weighed the sacks of potatoes or cotton with such speed that the worker couldn't see exactly how much his haul weighed. Then the contractor would deduct money for the ride in the labor bus and money for social security taxes. But the money for the taxes was never reported and would never be claimed since many of the workers were from Mexico.

The contractor would sell sodas and lunches to the workers at high prices. How Cesar and Richard were tempted by the

contractor's chant of, "Sodas! *¡Frescas!*" as they worked in 105-degree heat! Moreover, the contractors would lie about the nice labor camps where the workers would be living during harvesttime. But when they arrived in their old cars, they found muddy or dusty camps with one irrigation canal for their drinking and bath water, and outhouses that smelled terrible and buzzed with flies.

After 1938 Cesar worked in all kinds of crops. During all this time, the family lived in tents, the homes of family and friends, and labor camp shacks with no electricity, water, or plumbing. At times the family had nothing to eat. Wherever Cesar looked at the end of a day, the horizon was flat. Did he wonder if that was his future—the flatness of farmlands that ran for acres and acres? Would this be his life? Would this be all that he would know?

CHAPTER FOUR

A New Life

CESAR JOINED THE navy in the mid-1940s to experience something new. He stayed two years, then returned to California to help his family. He returned to the routine of migrating with the crops.

As he worked he had time to think about the injustices he had known. He recalled how he was forced to run laps in PE class for speaking Spanish, how he wasn't allowed in restaurants because he was Mexican American, and how he was arrested and put in jail because he dared to sit in the white section of a movie theater in Delano. He noticed that white people lived on one side of town and Mexicans on the other. He wondered why Mexicans had to work harder than most people. They had to wake up before dawn. They had to work stooped over for ten hours a day. They had to breathe in pesticides that stayed on leaves. There were no toilets. There was no clean water to drink. There were no rest breaks. Their whole day was just hard labor.

In 1948 Cesar married Helen Fabela, who was born in Brawley, California, but raised on a farm in the Delano area. They enjoyed a brief honeymoon visiting California missions. A couple of weeks later they were on their knees, cutting grapes. Later the newlyweds worked side by side in the cotton fields. Their marriage was happy, but their lives continued to include hard work in the fields.

It was about this time that Cesar noticed

that Mexican Americans like himself had begun to compete with Mexican immigrants for fieldwork. The Mexican workers were called *braceros*, which loosely translates to "worker's arms" in Spanish but translated into cheap labor for growers. Under a government program, *braceros* began to come into the United States from Mexico as guest workers during World War II when there was a labor shortage. They worked for lower wages than local Mexican Americans, Filipinos, and whites. Cesar had no problem with Mexican people; after all, his grandfather was from Mexico and, at heart, he was *puro Mexicano*. No, the problem was the growers' desire to squeeze out the most work for as little pay as possible. Cesar could see that the growers didn't care about the *braceros* once a crop was harvested. How and where they lived while working

23

didn't interest them either. He could see clearly how one group of poor people was being pitted against another more desperate group.

But Cesar kept working, this time share-cropping a strawberry field outside of San José. Their first child, Fernando, was a year old, and another was on its way.

CHAPTER FIVE

A Time to Learn

CESAR WENT AS far as the eighth grade, an accomplishment for a Mexican American in the 1930s. However, during the late 1940s and the early 1950s he got his true education. He met Catholic priests Donald McDonnell and Thomas McCullough and activist Fred Ross, all defenders of migrant workers. He learned that Pope Leo XIII supported a worker's right to organize a union. He read about Saint Francis of Assisi and Mahatma Gandhi, two pacifists. Pacifists are those who believe in nonviolence.

His informal education continued by way

Santa Clara County Library District
408-293-2326

Checked Out Items 3/25/2016 15:00
XXXXXXXXXX6589

Item Title	Due Date
1. Cesar Chavez : labor leader / David Seidman. 33305207577531	4/15/2016
2. Cesar Chavez / by Mary Olmstead. 33305211697861	4/15/2016
3. Cesar Chavez : a hero for everyone / by Gary Soto ; illustrated by Lori Lohstoeter. 33305207929211	4/15/2016

No of Items: 3

Amount Outstanding: $11.50

24/7 Telecirc: 800-471-0991
www.sccl.org
Thank you for visiting our library.

of example from his father, Librado. In his mid-fifties, Librado had neither money in the bank nor a permanent home to call his own. His health was frail because of an automobile accident. Despite this, he would stomp out of a field if a worker, even someone he didn't know, got upset with a contractor or grower. When the worker threw down his hoe or sack or knife and left the field, Librado's family followed out of principle.

One such moment occurred in 1947 when the Chavezes were picking cotton near Delano. Cesar looked up and locked his gaze on a long caravan of one-hundred-plus cars and trucks. Loudspeakers were blaring, "Strike! *¡Huelga!*" It was a caravan formed by the National Farm Labor Union (NFLU). Excited, the entire Chavez clan ran from the fields. They joined the strikers as they headed to Corcoran, where they rallied for two weeks.

There was a lot of racism in the San Joaquin Valley, where the town of Corcoran is. Mexicans, Filipinos, and poor whites were pushed around. They were even pushed out of the labor camps when they dared to use the word *strike*. It wasn't uncommon to see such evictees living on the sides of roads. Many were from Mexico, far from home. In a speech about a strike during the 1930s, a member of the Tulare County board of supervisors said: "Why, if I saw a Mexican dying in the street, I would not help him." Many people still had those feelings in the 1940s and 1950s.

The Chavez family returned to Delano in time to start cutting grapes. But Cesar stayed behind in Corcoran. He could see the power of a strike. It gave him hope.

Cesar's spirit was lifted further when he met Fred Ross, founder of the Community

Service Organization, known as the CSO. This organization was established in 1950 to help urban Mexican Americans in East Los Angeles. Later it grew, with chapters in Los Angeles, Hanford, Fresno, San José, Stockton, and other California towns and cities. Fred Ross hired Cesar to work for the CSO. Cesar started right away.

In 1958 and 1959, Cesar worked for the CSO in Oxnard, the place he had first seen the ocean. His job was to enroll people in citizenship classes and register them to vote.

Cesar liked this new job.

CHAPTER SIX

Organizing

CESAR RENTED A small office in Oxnard for his CSO job. He invited people to come discuss what was in their hearts. Right away he heard the fury of the local people about *braceros* taking their farm jobs, even the more skilled ones like driving a tractor. It was a delicate matter, one that caused Cesar to worry. He knew that the *braceros* were desperate for work, but the local Chicano workers were desperate as well. Cesar knew that something must be done.

Braceros were supposed to be employed only during a labor shortage. But there was no labor shortage in Oxnard or all of Ventura County. Locals would show up at the Farm Placement Center, where people went for day work. But none of them could get jobs, not even the men who had been in the armed services in World War II.

Cesar complained to the state government. When they didn't respond, he staged a "sit-in" on a bright but cool April day at the Jones Ranch. People sat right between the rows of tomato seedlings. As a *bracero* worked his short-handled hoe up or down a row, he eventually faced a local worker.

The sit-in came to an end when the county sheriffs and Highway Patrol arrived.

"Who's the leader?" a sheriff barked.

No one said anything. But an innocent mistake occurred; someone from the side of the road yelled, "Cesar, I got to tell you . . ."

That sentence was enough to point Cesar out. He and a few others were arrested for trespassing, but were soon released.

A month later Secretary of Labor James Mitchell was scheduled to stop in Ventura, a few miles from Oxnard. Cesar organized a protest. When Mitchell arrived at the airport, Cesar and a thousand people were waiting for him holding signs in the air that said "We Want Jobs." Mitchell hurried past the crowd, head down.

Later Cesar organized an evening march, with the protesters holding candles. Some of the candles sputtered or blew out in the wind, but they were all relit. The spirits of the local workers were also relit.

It was there, in Oxnard, that Cesar learned about the power of the march. It got people's attention. He also needed a symbol for the march, something people would remember. When a woman asked, "Can I bring my banner of Our Lady of Guadalupe?" a smile crossed his face. He used that banner for a march the next day. Mexican songs kept time with the strum of a guitar, and the thump of a *guitarrón*.

During the next few days he organized a march with thousands of people! The local Chicanos were not going to be silent anymore. All the while television crews were following this mass of people. Where were they going? They were walking toward Cesar's dream— somewhere better than seventy-five cents an hour for grueling work.

In the end all of Cesar's work paid off. Local Chicano workers got the farm jobs and better pay—it was increased to a dollar an hour. It wasn't a lot, but it was a start.

During his fifteen months in Oxnard, the community learned Cesar Chavez's name.

Mexican Americans grew bolder. They had learned that when they worked together, they could make a difference. This was all part of Cesar's legacy.

CHAPTER SEVEN

On His Own . . . with Others

The progress in Oxnard was short-lived. After Cesar left the area, CSO leaders began fighting among themselves, and all his work crumbled. He fumed when he learned that farmers returned to hiring *braceros*. Still, Cesar wouldn't give up. He wanted to organize farmworkers, because he knew they could get better pay if they were united. One worker alone couldn't do it, but hundreds together could bring change. They needed their own union. Cesar quit the CSO to build a union for farmworkers.

In 1962 he moved his family to Delano,

where he rented a small house for Helen and their eight children. Of course, Cesar was worried. He didn't have much money saved. But Helen was behind him. She was prepared to support his work for *la causa*.

He called up his cousin Manuel Chavez and told him he planned to start a new union. Manuel laughed and told Cesar he was crazy. A union for farmworkers! But Manuel was soon with him. So were Dolores Huerta and Gilbert Padilla, whom he had met through the CSO, plus other good people who would help.

While Cesar traveled up and down the San Joaquin Valley, talking to farm workers during house meetings, Helen worked in the fields around Delano. Sometimes she took their oldest son, Fernando, with her on the weekends. She rose before daylight. She dressed, prepared lunches for the children, and went

out to pick peas, bag onions, or pick grapes.

Money was tight that year, and would remain tight all their lives. One time Helen stopped at a Safeway store to pick up a few groceries. A contest was going on, a sort of lottery. With each purchase the shopper received a coupon, which she ran under a faucet to reveal the prize.

Helen took her coupon home and discovered she had won! A hundred dollars!

She could see herself buying shoes for the children. Maybe fabric to make dresses for the girls. But in the end, the money was used to pay the gas bill for Cesar's car.

Cesar didn't eat much when he traveled from town to town. One afternoon he was driving his old station wagon in Corcoran with his cousin Manuel. The two were hungry. They hadn't eaten in a day and a half. With his stomach rumbling, Manuel shouted at

Cesar, "I'm going to ask for food." He told Cesar to pull over.

Cesar was shocked. He wouldn't stoop to ask another person for food. Later he would call himself prideful. But Cesar did what Manuel asked. He pulled over in front of a house that was no more than a shack.

Cesar was embarrassed when Manuel knocked on the door. Manuel told the woman who answered that he and his friend didn't have any food. Could they have something to eat? The woman showed them inside and fed them. Later Cesar would say, "The poor are great."

The union began to come together quickly, and with hardly any money. Manuel Chavez borrowed $1.50 for gas and drove to Fresno to rent a place for their first convention. A smooth talker, he was able to get the use a rundown theater. He promised the owner he would pay for its use later.

On September 30, 1962, in that musty theater the union was officially born. It was called the National Farm Workers Association. There were two hundred members of this new union from all parts of California.

When the union's flag was revealed, the members were shocked. Cesar's brother Richard and his friend Andy Zermeño had designed a black eagle set against a red background. At first it seemed too strong, like it was a communist symbol. But the design was approved, along with the monthly dues of $3.50, plus a constitution that was accepted in early spring 1963.

CHAPTER EIGHT

"Huelga," Cesar Chants

THE FIRST TEST for the NFWA came in 1965 when, in Delano, the Filipinos walked off fields run by Schenley Industries. They were angry because their hourly wage was cut from $1.40 to $1.25. Chicanos' hourly wages were cut to $1.10—different wages for different racial groups! The Filipinos had their own union called the Agricultural Workers Organizing Committee (AWOC). In Delano, Larry Itliong ran the AWOC. At Filipino Hall, he announced a strike on September 8 just as the grapes were ripening.

"Join us, Cesar," Larry Itliong asked. The AWOC needed help.

Cesar hesitated because his NFWA had fewer than a thousand members. Of these, only a third were paying dues regularly. But when the NFWA met, they decided to join their fellow *compañeros* of the AWOC. A meeting was held at a church in Delano. Carloads of Mexican and Chicano farmworkers from the towns and camps arrived and voiced their support for the Filipinos. *La huelga*—"the strike"—began that evening, September 16, a symbolic date because it was Mexican Independence Day. *"¡Viva la causa!"*—"Long live the cause!"—was shouted. That evening it was shouted a lot, along with, *"¡Qué viva César Chávez!"*—"Cesar lives!"

Cesar and other leaders tried to get the growers to meet with them. The growers refused. Cesar then sent certified letters to the growers, asking them to talk. But still they didn't respond. When he spoke to the mayor of Delano, the mayor told Cesar he didn't want to get involved.

So on September 20 members of the NFWA and AWOC got up in the morning when it was still dark. Even the roosters weren't yet crowing. The strikers drove to Schenley Industries' 4000-acre farm. They posted strikers at different entrances and formed picket lines. Just after sunrise, when the first rooster began to crow, they began to shout, *¡Huelga! ¡Huelga! ¡Huelga!*" The workers who had started early peeked up curiously from the vines.

"It's a strike," someone shouted.

A few left the field and joined the strikers. Others went home because they could see trouble brewing. But most continued working, half-hidden behind the leaves of the grape vines tipped with dew that ran like tears.

A foreman arrived in a company truck to see about all the noise.

"What's this all about?" the foreman asked.

"We're striking!" someone answered.

The foreman mumbled and drove away. An hour later the Kern County sheriffs arrived in a cloud of dust. They merely watched the strikers that first day but eventually got involved. During the next six months the Kern County sheriffs would take thousands of pictures of the strikers and their supporters. They even questioned them. Both acts were an invasion of privacy. And within twenty-four hours of the initial picket on September 20, the FBI began following the strikers.

CHAPTER NINE

Fights in the Fields

CESAR WAS DETERMINED to follow the examples of Mahatma Gandhi and Martin Luther King Jr. Both of these leaders believed in nonviolence. Cesar told the strikers not to strike back in anger no matter what might happen.

For the most part the strikers controlled their emotions. But the farmers shouted angrily at the strikers; other times they tried to run over them with their trucks. One day an angry farmer grabbed *huelga* signs from the strikers. He cursed the strikers, then blasted the signs with his shotgun. Another day farmers beat Cesar and other strikers. But Cesar, ribs bruised, told the union members not to respond with violence.

The farmers grew angry those fall months of 1965. They unleashed insults on the strikers. A crop duster airplane buzzed the strikers and sprayed them with sulfur and pesticides. Dogs were let loose on the strikers. The sheriffs did nothing when foremen and ranchers stomped on the toes of the farmworkers. These bullies taunted the farmworkers by calling them "stupid Mex." The sheriffs themselves took down license plate numbers of cars parked on the sides of the fields. Later the drivers of these cars would be stopped by the police and harassed.

The Delano police shadowed Cesar and other union leaders. Every morning Helen would pull back the curtains and see a police car parked across the street. The police themselves didn't appear to be aware of the laws of free speech. At the W. B. Camp ranch forty-four strikers started yelling, *"Huelga! Huelga! Huelga!"* at the strikebreakers who had entered the fields to work. The county sheriff told them to stop, but the strikers kept yelling. All forty-four were arrested, including Helen Chavez and pastors from nearby churches. With bail set at $276, few could get out of jail. Only a court order released them. Yelling *"Huelga!"* was free speech. They could yell that word and *"Qué viva la causa"* all they wanted.

Delano suddenly was on the map. Reporters from as far away as New York City combed the streets. The labor strike was mentioned on the nightly news. Americans got to see for themselves how the farm workers lived when CBS presented "Harvest of Shame" on television. Perhaps some looked down at their dinner plates and thought: Farmworkers brought me this food.

Senator Robert F. Kennedy visited Delano. He toured the labor camps and was hurt to see so much poverty. He shook his head when he heard about an organization called Mothers Against Chavez. Even more shocking for him was learning that the average annual income for a farmworker was $2,400. How did people live?

The growers grumbled. If the local Chicano, Filipino, and Mexicans didn't want to work for what the growers believed was a fair wage, they would get others to take their place. During October labor contractors brought in Mexican workers to take the place of strikers. These workers felt bad when they realized a strike had been called. Still, two or three busloads of strikebreaking workers arrived daily from Mexico. They harvested the grapes. Once that was done, they were left to try to find work on their own. The large growers didn't care about the Mexican workers once the harvests were finished.

The large farmers started to use children as young as seven to help with the harvest. Their jobs were often to carry crates and boxes to their parents. Older children helped pick the grapes. They often worked in pesticide-tainted fields, putting their health at risk. There were labor laws that were supposed to protect children, but neither the sheriffs nor the foremen enforced them.

The large growers seemed greedy. For two and a half decades they had had the *bracero* program—cheap labor from Mexico. They had water paid for by the government. They had tax breaks. They had free research from the University of California. They wanted all these benefits for themselves. Yet they wouldn't share the abundance with the farm workers who did all the work.

With November came the rains and the Tule fog that smothered the valley in a gray shroud. The strike was still on, but there was nothing left to harvest, although a few strikebreakers tied vines in the icy mornings.

During December important labor leaders from across the country visited Delano. They wanted to see for themselves the large farms and the working conditions of the farmworkers. What they saw made them very upset. They were disgusted with the way the large growers treated the workers.

CHAPTER TEN

La Peregrinación

IN 1965 MARTIN Luther King Jr. was trying to stop segregation, the unfair treatment of black people, in the South. Cesar Chavez was also trying to work for social justice in the San Joaquin Valley. He knew that the big growers would have to be hurt financially before they would bargain. So he called for a boycott of Schenley Industries and the DiGiorgio Corporation. He asked Americans not to buy their products.

"Don't eat grapes," Cesar yelled through a bullhorn. He was at a Safeway store in Fresno explaining to the shoppers about the boycott. He would travel to Stockton, Sacramento, Modesto, Merced, and San Francisco. The message was the same: "Don't eat grapes."

He sent organizers who had never been out of rural California to faraway cities. They found themselves in New York, San Francisco, Detroit, and Chicago. They learned that America cared about the farmworkers' cause. In Boston, for instance, supporters marched with boxes of Delano grapes on their shoulders and dumped them in the harbor. Their protest was called the Boston Grape Party.

Cesar had another idea. He decided to take the protest a step farther by literally making his steps count. He would go on a three-hundred-mile *peregrinación*—"pilgrimage"— from Delano to Sacramento, California's state capital. The marches in Oxnard had been successful in getting people's attention. Why wouldn't it work here? The march would start in Delano and end at the steps of the capitol building on Easter Sunday. It was Lent, a time of sacrifice for Christians.

On March 17, 1966, at nine o'clock in the morning, union members and supporters gathered at the headquarters of the NFWA. It was a cool but clear day. Even before it started, a few people in passing cars clenched their fists in support. The Delano police were there too, eyeing them from across the street. They had been alerted that a march would take place.

The FBI was also there and even among the marchers. Every day an informant would file a report with the bureau in Los Angeles about the march.

Cesar arrived a little after eight in the morning. He was tired. He had stayed up most of the night, talking on the telephone to supporters in Sacramento and San Francisco. Cesar looked at the shoes the marchers were wearing. Some had work boots and others tennis shoes. He looked down at his own shoes. His were ordinary dress shoes, worn at the heels and already dusty, though he had yet to take a step. He saw that the marchers were prepared with hats, scarves to cover themselves against the wind and dust, and long-sleeved shirts to keep off the sun. Some wore sunglasses. There were flags and banners and arm bands that read NFWA. Angie Hernandez Herrera, the twenty-year-old daughter of Julio Hernandez, one of the first members of the union, started off at Cesar's side. She remained at his side during the entire twenty-five-day march.

"¡Nos vamos!" Cesar called. "Let's go!" But

he had to wonder if he could make it. He was out of shape. Three hundred miles was a long way.

They marched to Highway 99. They cut through downtown, where the march was briefly halted because the union didn't have a parade license. But the chief of police, smarting from bad press, let them continue. And they did. The original seventy-five marchers headed toward Richgrove, about eight miles northeast of Delano. They walked down a country road with a single yellow line down the middle. Cows mooed at them. Cars honked their support. Some drivers shouted cuss-words at them.

"Don't let them get you mad," Cesar advised. He wanted the pilgrimage to be peaceful.

Within the first five miles, Cesar's right

ankle became swollen and his steps painful. But he wouldn't stop. He walked a total of twenty-one miles that first day.

Cesar was glad to see the outskirts of Ducor, a town with fewer than two thousand residents. Everyone in that town kept to themselves. They were scared to greet the marchers. The farmers might not give them work, they feared. Only an elderly woman offered her home. The marchers slept on the living room floor and in the backyard under the stars. This elderly woman made up her own bed for Cesar. She knew that Cesar was doing something special.

The next day he woke up at four thirty. It was still dark. He soaked his feet and then dressed for the day. The next city was Porterville, a twenty-five-mile journey that was almost too much for Cesar. The bottoms of his feet were blistered. His right leg was swollen up to his knee. Angie Hernandez hooked her arm into his arm and told him to stay strong. That night he slept at Reverend James and Susan Drake's home in Porterville. With day two done, he was glad to have a nice shower and a bed to sleep in. Cesar had a fever and his right leg was swollen. His feet throbbed.

During this twenty-five-day march, hecklers in passing cars yelled insults at them. Some threw soda cans, eggs, and tomatoes. But most drivers tooted their horns in support and waved. At every town people would rush from their homes to give them sodas and food, rosaries, and prayer cards, and to ask about the strike. Just what are they doing? they eagerly wondered.

At each stop—Lindsay, Parlier, Chowchilla, and Manteca, among sixteen other places—

the marchers sang songs in the evening. *"De Colores"* became the union's unofficial anthem. It was a song of hope.

There was hope and special moments. One Sunday a poor family came out of their run-down house, yelling, *"¡Compañeros! ¡Compañeros! ¡Señor Chávez!"* One of the teenage daughters was walking carefully because she was balancing punch in a glass bowl. The other daughters were holding the cups. Cesar gratefully took a cup and drank. Cesar smiled and thanked the family for providing the marchers with the best they had.

Every day the original marchers—*los originales,* as they were called—picked up supporters. What was once a thin line now stretched for ten miles in places. The march made national headlines. In Chicago people marched through a Latino barrio in support.

Not everyone, however, seemed to care,

including California governor Edmund "Pat" Brown. He wasn't at the state capitol in Sacramento when the marchers arrived on Sunday, April 10. He was in Palm Springs, vacationing with singer Frank Sinatra. Cesar was disappointed. But he was happy to see a rally of nearly ten thousand farmworkers and supporters. Even before he began to speak, they were yelling, *"¡Qué viva la causa! ¡Qué viva César Chávez!"*

The best news was that Schenley Industries was ready to negotiate. They were ready to accept the union.

CHAPTER ELEVEN

The Fight on many Fronts

CESAR NEXT CONFRONTED DiGiorgio Corporation, which owned more than thirteen thousand acres of vineyards that spread throughout San Diego, Kern, Kings, Tulare, Fresno, and Merced counties. DiGiorgio also owned factories that canned fruits and vegetables.

Three days after the march to Sacramento, Cesar called for a boycott of products of the DiGiorgio Corporation. Right away the corporate leaders seemed willing to talk with the AWOC and NFWA. They appeared friendly, as if nothing was wrong. But on the day

65

union and corporate leaders met in San Francisco, Cesar broke off talks when he learned that security guards had beaten some of the strikers. He was really mad when he heard that Ofelia Diaz, a worker who had been with the company for about twenty-five years, was fired because she had asked some of her coworkers to consider joining the union.

Almost immediately the strike and boycott hurt the DiGiorgio Corporation. They were losing thousands of dollars every day. Their image was tarnished. All across the country people were cheering the farmworkers. Movie stars began to join the pickets— Jane Fonda, Leonard Nimoy, and Mary Tyler Moore were among them. To make themselves more powerful, the AWOC and NWFA united and became the United Farm Workers Organizing Committee (UFWOC). It was later renamed the United Farm Workers.

The DiGiorgio Corporation decided to become friendly with the Teamsters Union, which had begun talking to farmworkers in Borrego Springs, near San Diego, and Sierra Vista ranch, near Delano. The Teamsters were known for representing truckers and cannery workers. They now wanted to represent farmworkers.

The DiGiorgio Corporation arranged for busloads of farmworkers from Texas and Mexico to break the strike. But there was more. As soon as the farmworkers got off the bus, the corporation asked them to sign cards saying that they wanted the Teamsters to represent them. They signed because they were desperate for a job.

Teamsters and strikebreakers! Plus the courts limited the numbers of strikers that could be at the DiGiorgio Corporation farms and vineyards at a time. The success of the union looked bleak when just a month before they had been celebrating the Schenley Industries victory.

What now?

Cesar answered through action. The strikers and supporters caravanned to Borrego Springs farm. For a week they yelled for the strikebreakers to come out of the fields, to join the union. Some looked up, their eyes barely seen under their hats. They didn't want to get involved. On Monday, June 27, the strikers stood at the edge of the tractor path, yelling *"¡Huelga! ¡Huelga!"* About ten farmworkers stopped working and came out of the fields to shake hands with their *compañeros*, the strikers. They were convinced that the farmworkers' union was for them.

Two of the young men who left the fields were José Renteria and Juan Flores. They

approached Cesar. "Help us get our belongings back," José asked. Their stuff was at the camp where the strikebreakers lived.

Cesar thought this over. He figured that if these men were brave enough to leave their jobs, he could help them get their things back.

Cesar, José, and Juan, along with Chris Hartmire and Father Victor Salandini, drove Cesar's station wagon down a dusty path to the camp. When they got there, security guards confronted them. The guards raised their rifles and told them to stop and get out of the station wagon. They led Cesar and the others to a truck, where they were held for six hours in the scorching heat. The guards let Juan and José get their things and leave, but the others were forced to stay.

At ten o'clock that evening the county sheriffs came and chained Cesar, Chris

Hartmire, and Father Salandini in shackles. The three men were booked in San Diego for trespassing.

Farmworkers were outraged at the arrest. Supporters around the country were outraged too, when they learned that the sheriffs had put Cesar in chains. They sent letters to the governor and money to the union to help *la causa*. The three were given probation. The DiGiorgio Corporation looked bad. All Cesar was trying to do was retrieve Juan and José's belongings, and he ended up in jail.

Finally the DiGiorgio Corporation agreed to hold elections at the Sierra Vista ranch. Farmworkers would vote for the UFWOC, the Teamsters, or no representation at all.

"¡Sí se puede!" Cesar said. "We can do it!"

The union had much work to do. For two weeks Cesar and other leaders talked to farmworkers. They explained why a union would be good for them. They talked about wage increases, ten-minute breaks, toilets in the fields, a hospital clinic, a credit union, a nursery for children, and the pension they would receive at the end of their working years.

Elections were held on August 30, 1966. Cesar and the other leaders were nervous. The ballots were cast from early morning to late in the evening. One family had traveled in their old car from El Paso, Texas, to vote. The car, however, broke down, so they didn't arrive in time. The man broke down too. "If you lose by four votes, I'll never forgive myself," he said.

When the polls were closed, the ballots were driven to San Francisco in the trunk of a Highway Patrol car. Dolores Huerta followed that patrol car. The next day she called the headquarters in Delano. The union won! That night there was a party at Filipino Hall, where people celebrated by shouting, *"¡Viva la causa! ¡Viva César Chávez!"*

On September 22, Martin Luther King Jr. sent a telegram to Cesar Chavez. In part it read: "The fight for equality must be fought on many fronts—in the urban slums, in the sweat shops of the factories and fields. Our separate struggles are really one."

CHAPTER TWELVE

Hunger for *La Causa*

NEXT CESAR DECIDED to face the largest of all grape growers, the Giumarra family. The family owned nearly eleven thousand acres. The workers were looking for help, and Cesar believed that he could bring it to them.

On August 3, 1967, the Giumarra workers voted to strike. *"¡Bastante!"* they yelled. "Enough!" More than two-thirds of the workers walked off the job. Giumarra did as other large corporate farms had in the past: They brought in strikebreakers from Texas and Mexico. They got the courts to say that the union could only have a few strikers at each farm.

Cesar sent organizers across the country to spread the word not to buy Giumarra grapes. But the Giumarra farms were sneaky. They boxed and shipped their grapes under sixty different names. Shoppers in major cities couldn't tell the difference. They were confused. The union came up with a solution: Boycott all fresh California grapes.

"Don't eat grapes," Cesar told the nation.

Seven days a week Cesar was on the road. He talked to college students, labor leaders, school children, politicians, growers, consumers, and farmworkers—anyone who would listen.

While on the road, he was disturbed to hear that some union members weren't obeying his policy of nonviolence. He had set down this rule and had reminded them of the examples of Gandhi and Martin Luther King Jr.

But the strikers were getting impatient.

There had been some gains. But the farm-workers wanted solutions now!

They started throwing rocks at the strike-breakers. They rode motorcycles down the rows, tearing the paper grape trays. Some sheds were burned, an irrigation pump was blown up, and nails were thrown into the street to puncture the tires of police cars and company trucks. There were fistfights between strikers and some of the foremen of the Giumarra farms.

Cesar decided to fast until the union members and their supporters stopped the violence. Helen was against it, but realized that she couldn't change Cesar's mind.

Cesar began his fast on February 15, 1968, at Forty Acres, a place at the outskirts of Delano. He took a swig of Diet-Rite soda, his favorite drink. After that Cesar drank only water. He grew weak. Family and good friends were worried. They wondered how long could he last. A few of the union members were mad at him. There was so much work to do, and here he was in bed!

But Cesar was convinced that he had to fast. He wanted the union members and their supporters to stop their violence. He wanted them to stay strong and not give up, for some of the strikers had returned to work.

Cesar continued his fast in spite of pleas from Helen, family, and friends. He lost thirty pounds. On the thirteenth day of his fast he had to get out of bed and go to court in Bakersfield. The judge wanted to ask him why the strikers were still picketing the Giumarra farms when there was a court order for the union to stop.

The farmworkers knew that they seldom won in court. They knew that Cesar had been fasting for them. So over thousands of

farmworkers showed up at the courthouse in Bakersfield to show their support. It was foggy and cold. They prayed on their knees and crossed themselves when Cesar passed— he was so weak from fasting that he was held up by supporters.

About two hundred farmworkers followed Cesar and other union leaders into the courtroom. That was the first time many of them had ever been in a courtroom. When the lawyer for Giumarra asked that the farm workers be removed, the judge turned red with anger. "Well, if I kick these farmworkers out of the courthouse, it'll be another example of gringo justice!" he replied. The charges against Cesar and the union were dropped.

Cesar left the court and returned to his bed at Forty Acres, where he continued his fast. He continued to get weaker and weaker. The light in his eyes dimmed. Helen and their children worried that he would die. Senator Robert Kennedy sent a message asking Cesar to please stop fasting. He had gone twenty-one days without eating.

Cesar ended his fast on March 11, 1968, at a park in Delano, where a mass was celebrated with nearly eight thousand people who had gathered. Senator Kennedy was among them. The two of them sat together. Senator Kennedy handed Cesar a piece of bread blessed by a priest. Cesar put it into his mouth and chewed slowly. He was very weak. But his spirit was strong and grew even stronger when he heard someone shout, *"¡Qué viva César Chávez!"*

CHAPTER THIRTEEN

Onward, Adelante!

IT WAS SPRING 1968, and this was just the beginning. The union was growing in members just as the vines were beginning to droop with bunches of swelling grapes. It would win more contracts from large growers. What had started six years earlier as *la causa* for farmworkers now affected other Latinos. *La causa* stirred urban Chicanos to seek social change. Sadly that year two of the strongest leaders of the civil rights movement would be gunned down. The country wept for Martin Luther King Jr. and Senator Kennedy.

Cesar had begun a struggle for social justice

in the fields. He had known farm-work as a child and would know it all his life. For the next twenty-five years he would battle the rich and powerful that believed they should make the rules that the poor lived by. But they were wrong. Because of Cesar, the rules changed. He touched the lives of farmworkers and people throughout the country.

Cesar was willing to fast until he died. Some say that first fast, and two others, eventually cost him his life. He died in his sleep on April 23, 1993, in San Luis, Arizona, a small town not far from where he was born. His gravesite is the former rose garden at the union's headquarters in Keene, California, called *La Paz*. Next to him are buried his faithful dogs, Boycott and Huelga.

A half-dozen old rose bushes still stand near his grave. When the wind blows in late summer, the flowers scent the air. Often school buses bring children to see where Cesar lived and worked. They visit his grave. When they bend down with flowers for his simple headstone, they honor him and every farmworker who traveled down a long and dusty row.

Bibliography

Dunne, John Gregory. *Delano*. New York: Farrar, Straus and Giroux, 1967.

Ferriss, Susan, and Ricardo Sandoval. *Fight in the Fields*. New York: Harcourt Brace, 1997.

Levy, Jacques E. *Cesar Chavez: Autobiography of La Causa* New York: W. W. Norton & Company, 1975.

Loftis, Anne. *Witness to the Struggle*. Reno: University of Nevada Press, 1998.

London, Joan, and Henry Anderson. *So Shall Ye Reap*. New York: Thomas Y. Crowell, 1971.

Taylor, Paul. *On the Ground in the Thirties.* Layton, Utah: Peregrine Smith Books, 1983.

Taylor, Ronald B. *Chavez and the Farm Workers.* Boston: Beacon Press, 1975.

About the Author

GARY SOTO serves as the Young People's Ambassador for the California Rural Legal Assistance (CRLA) and the United Farm Workers of America (UFW). His other books include *Baseball in April and Other Stories*, *Cat's Meow*, and *The Old Man & His Door*. He lives in Berkeley, California.

MILESTONE BOOKS

Relive other Milestones in history.

A Three-Minute Speech:

Lincoln's Remarks at Gettysburg

By Jennifer Armstrong

Illustrated by Albert Lorenz

Nellie Bly:

A Name to Be Reckoned With

By Stephen Krensky

Illustrated by Rebecca Guay

Published by Simon & Schuster